Kitanai and Hungry Hare EAT HEALTHFULLY

by Thomas Kingsley Troupe

illustrated by Jamey Christoph

PICTURE WINDOW BOOKS
a capstone imprint

Kitanai the Origami Dog loved running through the garden. After his jog, he rested in the quiet shade beneath the plants.

One morning, the ground rumbled ...

Whoa! What was that?

Carrots

3

4

6

8

9

11

After breakfast Kitanai and Hungry had loads of energy. They barked and hopped until the sun was high in the sky.

What should I eat for lunch, little doggie?

Let's chop up some veggies and make a salad. Do you like carrots?

Of course!

13

The two spent the afternoon playing by the pond.
Soon the sun was sinking behind the trees.

I'm rumbling again.
Any dinner ideas?

Sure. Try a lean meat, like
turkey. Steam some peas,
or have beans with it.

16

Drink water as often as you can.

But I like soft drinks. There's water in those.

A little. But soda is loaded with sugar.

And too much sugar is bad, right?

Exactly! Your body needs lots of water. When you sweat or pee, you need to replace the water you lost.

19

GLOSSARY

calcium—a soft mineral needed for strong teeth and bones

delicious—tasty

grain—the seed of a cereal plant such as wheat, rice, corn, rye, or barley

protein—substance in food that helps keep muscles strong

READ MORE

Bellisario, Gina. *Choose Good Food!: My Eating Tips.* Minneapolis: Millbrook Press, 2014.

Bodden, Valerie. *Eating Healthy.* Healthy Plates. Mankato, Minn.: Creative Education, 2015.

Marsico, Katie. *Eat a Balanced Diet!* Your Healthy Body. Ann Arbor, Mich.: Cherry Lake Publishing, 2015.

INTERNET SITES

FactHound offers a safe, fun way to find Internet sites related to this book. All of the sites on FactHound have been researched by our staff.

Here's all you do:

Visit *www.facthound.com*

Type in this code: 9781479560820

Super-cool stuff!

Check out projects, games and lots more at
www.capstonekids.com

INDEX

breakfast, 10–11

dairy, 8, 11
dinner, 14–15

food groups, 8–9, 15
fruits, 6, 8, 10, 11, 16

grain, 8, 10, 11

lunch, 12

protein, 8, 11

snacks, 6, 9, 16–17

teeth, 17
treats, 17

vegetables, 6, 8, 12–13, 14, 15
vegetarians, 15

water, 18

Editor: Jeni Wittrock
Designer: Ashlee Suker
Art Director: Nathan Gassman
Production Specialist: Morgan Walters
The illustrations in this book were created digitally.

Picture Window Books are published by Capstone,
1710 Roe Crest Drive, North Mankato, Minnesota 56003
www.capstonepub.com

Library of Congress Cataloging-in-Publication
Troupe, Thomas Kingsley, author.
Christoph, Jamey, illustrator.
Kitanai and Hungry Hare Eat Healthfully / by Thomas Kingsley Troupe.
pages cm.—(Nonfiction Picture Books. Kitanai's Healthy Habits)
Summary: "Kitanai the dog teaches Hungry Hare how to eat
healthfully"—Provided by publisher.
Audience: Ages 5–7.
Audience: K to grade 3.
ISBN 978-1-4795-6082-0 (library binding)
ISBN 978-1-4795-6114-8 (paperback)
ISBN 978-1-4795-6118-6 (eBook PDF)
1. Nutrition—Juvenile literature. 2. Health—Juvenile literature. I. Title.
RA777.T73 2015
613.2083—dc23   2014029079

Printed in the United States of America,
002033

Other titles in this series:

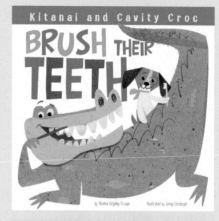

Kitanai and Cavity Croc
BRUSH THEIR TEETH
by Thomas Kingsley Troupe   Illustrated by Jamey Christoph

Kitanai and Filthy Flamingo
WASH UP
by Thomas Kingsley Troupe   Illustrated by Jamey Christoph

Kitanai and Lazy Lizard
GET FIT